WRITERS
ON ...
SEX

AMELIA CARRUTHERS

CONTENTS

Introduction   1

Antiquity: The Greeks & the Romans   9

The Renaissance   27

The Long Nineteenth Century   45

The Twentieth Century   61

Religion on Sex   73

Banned Books   89

Sex Letters   103

Forbidden Lust   113

Romantics vs. Realists   129

INTRODUCTION

Writing about sex is a famously difficult task. Yet despite this, literature has had a long, intimate and controversial relationship with the more *risqué* side of lovemaking. Throughout history many readers, writers and legislators have argued that any reference to this most basic of human needs will 'degrade' or 'lower the tone' of an otherwise respectable piece of literature. It has been the subject of censures from both ecclesiastic and secular courts, persecuted from *on-high* as well as by grass-roots campaigners. Aside from the familiar moral or stylistic concerns, it is also extremely difficult to draw a dividing line between the 'erotic' and the 'pornographic.' The former is seen as somehow more acceptable for a literary writer, whilst the latter is relegated to seedy backrooms and novels of questionable merit. The whole area is inherently subjective, steeped in personal, social, aesthetic, moral and religious values. Writing on sex can be comical as well as sinister, as varied, fascinating and pleasurable as the act is in reality. This anthology of *Writers on...* contains what could be construed as both the 'erotic' and the 'pornographic', so it is worthwhile to dwell on this important distinction a little longer.

The word 'erotic' has a long etymology, stemming from the Greek *erotikos* 'caused by passionate love, or referring to love', which in turn was a derivative of *eros;* one of the four main types of love, referring to 'sexual and/or romantic desire.' Thus *erotica* often depicts an *idealised* representation of the sexual act, generally celebrating or exalting in its effects. Pornography on the other hand (though these boundaries are incredibly hard to define in reality) frequently appeals *exclusively* to our senses and carnal appetites, with the immediate purpose of 'turning-on' the reader. Whilst both erotica and pornography can be equally explicit, and may produce the same result, it is the *intention* of the author that is key. Pornography's etymology reflects this modern usage; a combination of the Greek *porne* (prostitute) and *graphein* (write), i.e. *pornographos* – 'writing about prostitutes.' The term was first used in mid-nineteenth century Britain, when the rise of prostitution directly contrasted with the outwardly moral values of the Victorian era. Famous examples of the genre included Daniel Defoe's *Moll Flanders* (1722), and Jack Saul's *The Recollections of a Maryanne* (1881); a pioneering work of gay sexual fiction, chronicling the experiences of a London rent-boy.

Regardless of the controversial nature of this material, circulation of erotic literature was not seen as a major problem before the invention of printing, as the costs of producing individual manuscripts limited distribution to a very small group of readers. The invention of the printing press in the fifteenth century brought with it both a greater market and increasing restrictions, specifically censorship and legal restraints on grounds of obscenity. *Erotic* or *pornographic* literature had a much longer history however, and many sexual poems, prose and isolated musings have survived from Ancient Greece and Rome, including Sappho of Lesbos's lyrical poetry, Lucretius's poem *On the Passion of Love* and Ovid's celebrated *Ars Amatoria*, 'The Art of Love' – an early sex manual giving advice to any would-be lotharios. The *Ars Amatoria*'s first volume was written purely for men, however Ovid soon rectified this, producing a manual for women on how to attract *and keep* a man. He stated: 'I have just armed the Greeks against the Amazons; now, Penthesilea, it remains for me to arm thee against the Greeks.' The Indian *Kama Sutra* (written between 400 BCE and 200 CE) remains the world's best-known tome on sexual behaviour, widely considered to be the standard work on the subject. Yet contrary to popular perception, it is not *merely* a sex manual; it presents itself as a guide to a virtuous and gracious living, discussing the nature of love, pleasure, and family life. 'Kama' which is one of the four goals of Hindu life, means desire – including sexual desire, the latter being the subject of the textbook, and 'sutra' literally means a thread or line that holds things together.

Such works, ranging from the bawdy (Chaucer's *Millers Tale*) to the philosophical (Boccaccio's *Decameron*) continued throughout the medieval period, and were re-appropriated with gusto in the Renaissance. Authors such as

Walter Raleigh, John Donne and Andrew Marvell all produced stunning poetry on a sexual theme, but William Shakespeare's sonnets are perhaps the finest example of the genre's conflicted character. Dedicated to one 'Mr. W. H.' and not originally written for publication, they deal with themes such as the passage of time, love, beauty and mortality, expressing universalised and timeless reflections on our relationship with sex:

On purpose laid to make the taker mad;
Mad in pursuit and in possession so;
Had, having, and in quest to have, extreme;
A bliss in proof, and proved, a very woe.

As already noted, the emergence of cheap printing and publication methods saw erotic literature take on new meaning in the public mind. In the seventeenth century, John Wilmot, Earl of Rochester (1647-80) was notorious for his obscene verses, many of which were published posthumously in compendiums of poetry by him and other Restoration rakes. Such was the popular appeal of his works that Rochester's name was used as a selling point by publishers of erotic verse for centuries after. The rise of the novel in eighteenth century England provided a new medium for erotica. One of the most famous in this new genre was *Fanny Hill* (1748) by John Cleland. This book set a new standard in literary lewdness and was often adapted for the cinema in the twentieth century. Perhaps more daring than their English counterparts though, were the French writers of the time, many of whom were inspired by the first European translation of *Arabian Nights* in 1704. The climax of this trend is represented in the Marquis de Sade, whose works such as *120 Days of Sodom* (1785) and *Justine, or the Misfortunes of Virtue* (1788) were exemplars of the theme of sado-masochism. Indeed, the Marquis gave his name to the modern term 'sadism' whilst his later Austrian counterpart, Leopold von Sacher-Masoch provided the inspiration for 'masochism.' The French emperor Napoleon was so shocked by *Justine* that he described it as 'the most abominable book ever engendered by the most depraved imagination' and consequently ordered the arrest of de Sade who spent the last thirteen years of his life in prison.

Towards the end of the nineteenth century, a more 'cultured' form of erotica began to appear, by writers such as Algernon Charles Swinburne who pursued themes of paganism, lesbianism and sado-masochism in *Lesbia Brandon* (1859-68) and in contributions to *The Whippingham Papers* (1888). The work of D.H. Lawrence in turn, was inspired by the Scots dialect poems of Robert Burns, the bawdiest of which were collected in *The Merry Muses of Caledonia*. 'Sex' as we understand the term today, did not even exist until 1899, when H.G. Wells used it in *Love and Mr Lewisham* as an abbreviation for 'sexual intercourse.' It was not until 1928 and Lawrence's notorious *Lady Chatterley's Lover* that the term 'have sex' with someone was introduced. Under the widened scope of the Obscene Publications Act of 1857, many such classics of world literature were censored, aptly demonstrating that what is alluring to one person, may be distasteful, obscene or repulsive to another. Emile Zola, James Joyce and D.H. Lawrence all suffered prohibitions, and even medical textbooks such as those by Havelock Ellis were temporarily banned. When the unexpurgated edition of *Lady Chatterley's Lover* was finally published in 1960, it represented a victory for freedom of expression – and has since brought on a slew of sensual, erotic, and pornographic literature.

The modern proliferation of *sex in writing* has if anything, prompted a backlash against what is now seen as unnecessary and inartistic additions. This new found freedom to express one's erotic imaginings has, to bring this introduction full-circle, led many critics to question the literary merits of such depictions. Now that 'sex sells', what is there to separate imaginative and beautiful erotica from objectifying and simply animalistic pornographic depictions? In the end, nothing – because it is all in the *approach*, of the writer, and equally the reader. Presented in the right way, both can be equally mesmerising. One need only compare the lascivious letters of James Joyce to his wife Nora, and the metaphorical bliss of *Ulysses's* Leopold Bloom to realise that both can be just as troubling, uplifting and intrinsically carnal as the other. Nonetheless, what this collection will hopefully demonstrate, is the intrinsic value of literary reflections on this integral aspect of human life. Without the all-pervading nature of sex, it is very hard to imagine the intensity of Voltaire's *Candide*, Oscar Wilde's *Dorian Gray*, or Lord Byron's poetry or Shakespeare's plays. As Henry Louis Mencken put it, 'life without sex might be safer, but it would be unbearably dull.'

ANTIQUITY: THE GREEKS & THE ROMANS

With his venom

Irresistible

and bittersweet

that loosener

of limbs, Love

reptile-like

strikes me down.

– Saphho, (*c.*630-570 BCE) 'With His Venom.' Sappho was a Greek lyric poet born
on the island of Lesbos. The bulk of her poetry, which was greatly admired through
much of antiquity, has been lost, however her immense reputation has endured through
surviving fragments.

It is with our passions, as it is with fire and water, they are good servants but bad masters.

– Aesop (620-564 BCE), the Ancient Greek fabulist and author of *Aesop's Fables*.

Socrates: True love can have no contact with this sexual pleasure, and lovers whose love is true must neither of them indulge in it.

Glaucon: They certainly must not, Socrates.

Socrates: And so, I suppose you will lay down laws in the state we are founding, that will allow a lover to associate with his boy-friend and kiss him and touch him, if he permits it, as a father does his son, if his motives are good; but require that his association with anyone he's fond of must never give rise to the least suspicion of anything beyond this, otherwise he will be thought a man of no taste or education.

Glaucon: That is how I should legislate.

– Plato (*c.* 428/423-348 BCE), *The Republic,* 'Book III' (*c.* 380 BCE); a Socratic dialogue concerning the just governance of an ideal city-state.

I understand from you that your natural disposition is too much inclined toward sexual passion. Follow your inclinations as you will provided only that you neither violate the laws, disturb well-established customs, harm any one of your neighbours, injure your own body, nor waste your possessions. That you be not checked by some one of these provisos is impossible; *for a man never gets any good from sexual passion, and he is fortunate if he does not receive harm.*

– Epicurus (*c.* 341-271 BCE), an Ancient Greek philosopher and the founder of the 'Epicurean' school of philosophy – writing to one of his disciples. *Epicureanism* held that 'pleasure' was the greatest good, but the way to attain such pleasure was to live modestly and limit one's desires.

[He will crave]... For love also (as Homer says) if he is young and lusty; but not every one craves for this or that kind of nourishment or love, nor for the same things. Hence such craving appears to be our very own. Yet it has of course something natural about it; for different things are pleasant to different kinds of people, and some things are more pleasant to every one than chance objects. Now in the natural appetites few go wrong, and only in one direction, that of excess...

– Aristotle (384 – 322 BCE). The *Nicomachean Ethics* is Aristotle's most detailed discussion on the issues of love, sex and morality. Like the Stoics and Epicureans, Aristotle saw 'moderation' as key; the 'golden mean' between the extremes of excess and deficiency.

Philaenium: Do Give me another naughty kiss before we part.

Demaenetus: Go to hell!

[...]

Epilogue *(Spoken by the Company)*

If this old gentleman has indulged his inclinations a bit without informing his wife, he has done nothing new or strange, or different from what other men ordinarily do. No one has such an iron nature, such an unyielding heart, as not to do himself a good turn whenever he has any chance. So now in case you wish to beg the old fellow off from a beating, we opine that you can succeed, if you – give us some loud applause!

   – Titus Maccius Plautus (*c.* 254-184 BCE), whose comedies (such as *Asinaria*, 'The One with the Asses', quoted above) are the earliest surviving intact works of Latin literature.

The Passion of Love

This craving 'tis that's Venus unto us:
From this, engender all the lures of love,
From this, O first hath into human hearts
Trickled that drop of joyance which ere long
Is by chill care succeeded. Since, indeed,
Though she thou lovest now be far away,
Yet idol-images of her are near
And the sweet name is floating in thy ear.
But it behooves to flee those images;
And scare afar whatever feeds thy love;
And turn elsewhere thy mind; and vent the sperm,
Within thee gathered, into sundry bodies,
Nor, with thy thoughts still busied with one love,
Keep it for one delight, and so store up
Care for thyself and pain inevitable.

– Lucretius (99-55 BCE) was a Roman poet and philosopher. His only known work is
the epic philosophical poem, *De Rerum Natura,* quoted above ('Book IV'). It aimed to
explain Epicurean philosophy to a Roman audience, and depict a universe guided by
fortuna ('chance') and not the divine intervention of the traditional Roman deities.

Bringing love and wine together is adding fuel to the fire ... If you really want to know what she [or he] is like, look at her by daylight, and when you're sober.

– Ovid (43 BCE – *c*.18 CE), relationship advice from *Ars Amatoria*, 'The Art of Love', written in 2 CE.

Weep, you girls. My penis has given you up. Now
it penetrates men's behinds. Goodbye, wondrous
femininity!

(Bar/Brothel of Innulus and Papilio)

Restitutus says: 'Restituta, take off your tunic, please,
and show us your hairy privates.'

(Peristyle of the Tavern of Verecundus)

Amplicatus, I know that Icarus is buggering you.

Salvius wrote this.

(House of the Citharist)

I screwed the barmaid.

(Bar of Athictus)

– Roman Graffiti from the town of Pompeii (buried with the eruption of Mount Vesuvius in 79 CE)

Eyelashes fall out from excessive sex and so it is especially important for women to keep their eyelashes long to prove their chastity.

– Pliny the Elder (23-79 CE), a Roman author and naturalist who wrote the *Naturalis Historia* – which has since become a model for all other encyclopaedias. Pliny died in 79 CE while attempting the rescue (by ship) of a friend and his family from Pompeii.

... You know that many censure boy-loves for their instability, and jeeringly say that that intimacy like an egg is destroyed by a hair, for that boy-lovers like Nomads, spending the summer in a blooming and flowery country, at once decamp then as from an enemy's territory... But this charge cannot justly be brought against genuine lovers, and it was prettily said by Euripides, as he embraced and kissed handsome Agatho whose beard was just sprouting, that the Autumn of beautiful youths was lovely as well as the Spring. And I maintain that the love of beautiful and chaste wives flourishes not only in old age amid grey hairs and wrinkles, but even in the grave and monument. And while there are few such long unions in the case of boy-loves, one might enumerate ten thousand such instances of the love of women, who have kept their fidelity to the end of their lives.

– Plutarch (46-120 CE), *On Love* (date unknown). Pederasty was a firmly established Greek tradition of erotic relationships between adult males (the erastes) and younger males (the eromenos), the latter usually in their early teens. Debates over the relative merits of homosexual and heterosexual love were commonplace in this period, with equally strong views on either side. Plutarch himself was an advocate of heterosexual married love.

Certain young men with no long experience in the ancient literature were attacking Epicurus on the ground that he had introduced in his *Symposium* an unseemly and unnecessary discussion about the proper time for coition. For an older man to talk about sex in the presence of youths at a dinner-party and weigh the pros and cons of whether one should make love before dinner or after dinner was, they claimed, the extreme of indecency. At this, some of our company brought up Xenophon, who, so to speak, took his guests home after dinner, not on foot, but on horseback, to make love to their wives.

– Plutarch, *Table Talk* (date unknown). Many Ancient Greeks attacked Epicurus for his seemingly 'improper' philosophy of pleasure, though just as many supported him. Xenophon of Athens was a great historian and student of Socrates, famed for his depiction of the *Peloponnesian War*.

THE SEXUAL EMBRACE
CAN ONLY BE COMPARED
WITH MUSIC AND WITH
PRAYER.

– Marcus Aurelius (121-180 CE), Roman Emperor from 161-180 CE, and the last of the
'Five Good Emperors.' Marcus Aurelius is also considered one of the most important
Stoic philosophers.

Every animal is sad after coitus except the human female and the rooster.

– Galen of Pergamon (129-216 CE), a prominent Greek physician, surgeon and philosopher in the Roman empire; as well as the founder of 'Galenic Medicine.' His theories were followed by medical students well into the nineteenth century.

For the feeling of pleasure is not at all a necessity, but the accompaniment of certain natural needs – hunger, thirst, cold, sexual union.

– Clement of Alexandria (*c.* 150-215 CE), a Christian theologian influenced by Hellenistic philosophy (particularly Plato and the Stoics). This extract comes from the *Stromata* (*c.* 198-203 CE), the third in a trilogy of works on Christian life. Clement titled this work *Stromateis*, 'patchwork', because it deals with such a variety of matters.

SEXUAL LOVE IS A DESIRE WHICH DOES NOT AFFLICT VIRTUOUS MEN.

– Diogenes Laërtius (third Century CE), *Lives of Eminent Philosophers*. According to Laërtius, the Stoics held that 'wise men should have their wives in common, so that anyone might make love to any woman.' The Stoics taught that destructive emotions (i.e. romantic jealousy) resulted from errors in judgment, and that a 'sage', or person of 'moral and intellectual perfection', would not suffer such emotions.

THE RENAISSANCE

The wife must be with her face upwards towards the heavens, and the husband with his face downwards; this will facilitate pregnancy. But how shocking when, by means of diabolical habits and notions, married people do the reverse!

– Brother Cherubino de Siena (who lived during the fifteenth century), *Rules of Married Life* (*c.* 1490), on 'The correct position for the Matrimonial act.'

It is better to be bold than too circumspect, because fortune is of a sex which likes not a tardy wooer and repulses all who are not ardent.

– Niccolò Machiavelli (1469-1527), *The Prince*, 'Chapter XXV' (published 1532). The relationship between *fortuna* (the goddess of fortune, derived from classical Roman mythology) and free will is one of the most interesting philosophical problems posed by the text.

Whoso list to hunt, I know where is an hind,
But as for me, alas, I may no more;
The vain travail hath wearied me so sore,
I am of them that furthest come behind.
Yet may I by no means my wearied mind
Draw from the deer, but as she fleeth afore
Fainting I follow; I leave off therefore,
Since in a net I seek to hold the wind.
Who list her hunt, I put him out of doubt,
As well as I, may spend his time in vain.
And graven with diamonds in letters plain,
There is written her fair neck round about,
'*Noli me tangere*, for Caesar's I am,
And wild for to hold though I seem tame.'

– Thomas Wyatt (1503-1542), 'Whoso List to Hunt.' Wyatt was a lyrical poet credited
with introducing the sonnet into English literature. None of Wyatt's poems were
published during his lifetime however. The first book to feature his verse, *Tottel's
Miscellany* of 1557, was printed a full fifteen years after his death.

Make little pills ... of burnt alum and mastic with a little vitriol and orpiment.
Make them into very fine powder, that you can scarce feel them ... let them dry,
being pressed thin, and lay them on the mouth of the matrix, where it was first
broken open. Change it every six hours, always fomenting the place with rain
or cistern water. ... [After twenty-four hours] it will here and there make little
bladders, which being touched, will bleed much blood, that she can hardly be
known from a maid. ... [Alternately,] inject the dried blood of a hare or pigeon,
which being moistened by the moisture of the matrix, shows like live, fresh blood.

– Giambattista Della Porta (1535-1615), *Magiae Naturalis* ('Natural Magic'), first
published in 1558. Porta was an Italian scholar, living in Naples at the height of the
Scientific Revolution and the Reformation. The passage above concerns 'How to make a
virgin of a deflowered woman.'

I protest that the very cause that moved me to let forth this book, is not to encourage those wretches that wallow in the sin of fornication, but to admonish them speedily to amend their lives, lest the Lord God in His just wrath do one day make the disease to be incurable. This pestilent infection of filthy lust is a sickness very loathsome, odious, troublesome and dangerous, which spreadeth itself throughout all England and overfloweth as I think the whole world.

– William Clowes (1543-1604), an early English surgeon – producing one of the first ever written accounts of syphilis in *De Morbo Gallico*, published in 1579.

So sweet and delicious do I become,

when I am in bed with a man

who, I sense, loves and enjoys me,

that the pleasure I bring excels all delight,

so the knot of love, however tight

it seemed before, is tied tighter still.

– Veronica Franco (1546-1591), 'Franco's Response to Capitolo: I'. Franco was an Italian
poet and courtesan of sixteenth century Venice. The extract above comes from her
Terze Rime (published 1575), which contained eighteen verse epistles by Franco as well as
seven men writing in her praise.

The daughter-in-law of Pythagoras said that a woman who goes to bed with a man ought to lay aside her modesty with her skirt, and put it on again with her petticoat.

After mature deliberation of counsel, the good Queen to establish a rule and immutable example unto all posterity, for the moderation and required modesty in a lawful marriage, ordained the number of six times a day as a lawful, necessary and competent limit.

– Michel de Montaigne (1533-1592), a French philosopher, author and nobleman, famed for his *Essais* (1580). The first observation comes from an essay, 'Of the Power of Imagination' whilst the second comes from 'Upon Some Verses of Virgil.'

In summer's heat, and mid-time of the day,
To rest my limbs upon a bed I lay;
One window shut, the other open stood,
Which gave such light as twinkles in a wood,
Like twilight glimpse at setting of the sun,
Or night being past, and yet not day begun;
Such light to shamefaced maidens must be shown,
Where they may sport, and seem to be unknown:
Then came Corinna in a long loose gown,
Her white neck hid with tresses hanging down,
Resembling fair Semiramis going to bed,
Or Lais of a thousand wooers sped.
I snatched her gown; being thin, the harm was small,
Yet strived she to be covered therewithal;
And striving thus, as one that would be cast,
Betrayed herself, and yielded at the last.
Stark naked as she stood before mine eye,
Not one wen in her body could I spy.
What arms and shoulders did I touch and see,
How apt her breasts were to be pressed by me!
How smooth a belly under her waist saw I,
How large a leg, and what a lusty thigh!
To leave the rest, all liked me passing well;
I clinged her naked body, down she fell:
Judge you the rest: being tired she bade me kiss;
Jove send me more such afternoons as this.

– Christopher Marlowe's famed translation of Ovid's *Elegia V: Corinnae Concubitus*
(published posthumously in 1602). Marlowe (1564-1593) was the foremost Elizabethan
tragedian of his day and greatly influenced William Shakespeare.

Nay, but to live

In the rank sweat of an enseamed bed,

Stew'd in corruption,

honeying and making love

Over the nasty sty –

– William Shakespeare (1564-1616), *Hamlet*, Act III, scene 4 (published 1602).
Hamlet admonishing his mother, the Queen, on her proposed marriage to Claudius
(Hamlet's uncle).

He eats nothing but doves, love, and that breeds hot
blood, and hot blood begets hot thoughts, and hot
thoughts beget hot deeds, and hot deeds is love.

– William Shakespeare. Paris speaking in *Troilus and Cressida,* Act III, scene I
(published 1603).

The expense of spirit in a waste of shame

Is lust in action; and till action, lust

Is perjured, murderous, bloody, full of blame,

Savage, extreme, rude, cruel, not to trust,

Enjoy'd no sooner but despised straight,

Past reason hunted, and no sooner had

Past reason hated, as a swallow'd bait

On purpose laid to make the taker mad;

Mad in pursuit and in possession so;

Had, having, and in quest to have, extreme;

A bliss in proof, and proved, a very woe;

Before, a joy proposed; behind, a dream.

   All this the world well knows; yet none knows well

   To shun the heaven that leads men to this hell.

– William Shakespeare, 'Sonnet 129' published as part of *Shakespeare's Sonnets* in 1609.
This poem forms part of 'The Dark Lady' sequence, which distinguishes itself from the
'Fair Youth' sequence by being overtly sexual in its passion.

Wrong not, sweet empress of my heart,
The merit of true passion,
With thinking that he feels no smart,
That sues for no compassion;

Since, if my plaints serve not to approve
The conquest of thy beauty,
It comes not from defect of love,
But from excess of duty.

For, knowing that I sue to serve
A saint of such perfection,
As all desire, but none deserve,
A place in her affection,

I rather choose to want relief
Than venture the revealing;
Where glory recommends the grief,
Despair distrusts the healing.

– Walter Raleigh (1552-1618), 'The Silent Lover' (date unknown). Raleigh was an English
   aristocrat, writer, poet, soldier, spy, explorer – and court favourite of Queen Elizabeth I.

Twice or thrice had I lov'd thee,
Before I knew thy face or name;
So in a voice, so in a shapeless flame
Angels affect us oft, and worshipp'd be;
Still when, to where thou wert, I came,
Some lovely glorious nothing I did see.
But since my soul, whose child love is,
Takes limbs of flesh, and else could nothing do,
More subtle than the parent is
Love must not be, but take a body too;
And therefore what thou wert, and who,
I bid Love ask, and now
That it assume thy body, I allow,
And fix itself in thy lip, eye, and brow.

Whilst thus to ballast love I thought,
And so more steadily to have gone,
With wares which would sink admiration,
I saw I had love's pinnace overfraught;
Ev'ry thy hair for love to work upon
Is much too much, some fitter must be sought;
For, nor in nothing, nor in things
Extreme, and scatt'ring bright, can love inhere;
Then, as an angel, face, and wings
Of air, not pure as it, yet pure, doth wear,
So thy love may be my love's sphere;
Just such disparity
As is 'twixt air and angels' purity,
'Twixt women's love, and men's, will ever be.

– John Donne (1572-1631), 'Air and Angels' from *Songs and Sonnets* published in 1633.
Donne was a celebrated English poet and cleric in the Church of England. In this verse,
he resurrects the legitimacy of sensuous, bodily love.

Now therefore, while the youthful hue
Sits on thy skin like morning dew,
And while thy willing soul transpires
At every pore with instant fires,
Now let us sport us while we may,
And now, like amorous birds of prey,
Rather at once our time devour
Than languish in his slow-chapped power.
Let us roll all our strength and all
Our sweetness up into one ball,
And tear our pleasures with rough strife
Thorough the iron gates of life:
Thus, though we cannot make our sun
Stand still, yet we will make him run.

– Andrew Marvell (1621-1678), an English metaphysical poet and friend of John Milton.
'To His Coy Mistress' (written in the early 1650s) is considered one of Marvell's finest
works, addressing a woman who has been slow to respond to his sexual advances.

Now piercèd is her virgin zone;
She feels the foe within it.
She hears a broken amorous groan,
The panting lover's fainting moan,
Just in the happy minute.
Frighted she wakes, and waking, frigs.
Nature thus kindly eased
In dreams raised by her murmuring pigs
And her own thumb between her legs,
She's innocent and pleased.

– John Wilmot, 2nd Earl of Rochester (1647-1680), 'Song to Cloris', which tells the tale of a young pigherd's dreams of 'dirty sex.' Rochester was part of the Restoration era, which reacted against the 'spiritual authoritarianism' of the Puritan age before it. He was the embodiment of his epoch, just as well known for his rakish lifestyle as his poetry – though the two were often interlinked. Rochester died from venereal disease at the age of thirty-three.

THE LONG
NINETEENTH
CENTURY

You *need* us, you *adore* us, you're suffering for us. You want everything–
except to know what we think. You look deep in our eyes–and put your hand
up our dress. You call us, *'Pretty thing.'* That confuses us. The most beautiful
woman, the highest ranked, lives half dazzled by constant attention, half stifled by
obvious contempt. We think all we're good for is pleasing you–till one day, long
acquaintance with you dispels the last mist. In a clear light, we suddenly see you
as you are–and generally we start preferring ourselves. At thirty, I could finally say
no–or really say yes. That's when you begin backing away from us. Now I'm full-
grown. I pursue my happiness the same as any man.

– Pierre Beaumarchais (1731-1799), *La Folle Journée, ou Le Mariage de Figaro* ('The Mad
Day, or The Marriage of Figaro'), written in 1778. The play's denunciation of aristocratic
privilege has often been characterised as foreshadowing the French Revolution.

Yestreen I wed a lady fair,

And ye wad believe me,

On her cunt there grows nae hair,

That's the thing that grieves me.

It vexed me sair, it plagu'd me sair,

It put me in a passion,

To think that I had wad a wife,

Whase cunt was out o' fashion.

– Robert Burns (1759-1796), Scotland's national poet who along with such classics as 'Ault Lang Syne' and 'My Love is Like a Red Red Rose' also penned many cheeky and bawdy songs throughout his life. They were collectively published in *The Merry Muses of Caledonia* in 1800.

And again she began to caress me and kiss me; finally she drew me down on the little divan.

'You seem to be pleased with yourself in furs', she said. 'Quick, quick, give them to me, or I will lose all sense of dignity.'

I placed the furs about her, and Wanda slipped her right arm into the sleeve.

'This is the pose in Titian's picture. But now enough of joking. Don't always look so solemn, it makes me feel sad. As far as the world is concerned you are still merely my servant; you are not yet my slave, for you have not yet signed the contract. You are still free, and can leave me any moment. You have played your part magnificently. I have been delighted, but aren't you tired of it already, and don't you think I am abominable? Well, say something—I command it.'

'Must I confess to you, Wanda?' I began.

'Yes, you must.'

'Even it you take advantage of it', I continued, 'I shall love you the more deeply, adore you the more fanatically, the worse you treat me. What you have just done inflames my blood and intoxicates all my senses.' I held her close to me and clung for several moments to her moist lips.

'Oh, you beautiful woman', I then exclaimed, looking at her. In my enthusiasm I tore the sable from her shoulders and pressed my mouth against her neck.

'You love me even when I am cruel', said Wanda, 'now go!—you bore me—don't you hear?'

She boxed my ears so that I saw stars and bells rang in my ears.

'Help me into my furs, slave.'

– Leopold von Sacher-Masoch (1836-1895), *Venus in Furs* (1870), an Austrian writer and journalist who gave his name to 'Masochism.' The novel was a pioneering text, exposing the world of female dominance and sadomasochism. Many of the characters and themes were drawn heavily from Sacher-Masoch's own life.

Now, with your happy arms her waist surround,
Fond–grasping; on her swelling bosom now
Recline your cheek, with eager kisses press
Her balmy lips, and, drinking from her eyes
Resistless love, the tender flame confess,
Ineffable but by the murmuring voice
Of genuine joy; then hug and kiss again,
Strech'd on the flow'ry turf, while joyful glows
Thy manly pride, and, throbbing with desire,
Pants earnest, felt thro' all the obstacles
That interveen: but love, whose fervent course
Mountains nor seas oppose, can soon remove
Barriers so slight. Then when her lovely limbs,
Oft lovely deem'd, far lovelier now beheld,
Thro' all your trembling joints increase the flame,
Forthwith discover to her dazzled sight
The stately novelty, and to her hand
Usher the new acquaintance.

– John Armstrong (1709-1797), a Scottish physician, poet and satirist. 'The Oeconomy of
Love' (1791) – an eighteenth century 'poetical essay' and guide to sex.

Women are systematically degraded by receiving the trivial attentions which men think it manly to pay to the sex, when, in fact, men are insultingly supporting their own superiority.

– Mary Wollstonecraft (1759-1797), *A Vindication of the Rights of Woman*, 'Chapter IV' (1792); in which she argues that women are not naturally inferior to men, but appear to be only because they lack education.

The details... O God! ... I cannot find words to paint them. It was as if the villain, the most libertine of the four, though seemingly the least removed from the views of Nature, was prepared to tread her path and put a smaller degree of nonconformity into his order of worship, only by compensating for a semblance of lesser depravity by inflicting the highest degree of outrage upon my person.

Justine: Or Good Conduct Well-Chastised (1788)

What does one want when one is engaged in the sexual act? That everything around you give you its utter attention, think of only you, care only for you... every man wants to be a tyrant when he fornicates.

Philosophy in the Boudoir (1795)

– Marquis de Sade (1740-1814), a French aristocrat and revolutionary politician, famous for his libertine sexuality. He is best known for his erotic works, combining philosophical discourse with pornography, often depicting extremely violent sexual fantasies. Napoleon was so shocked by 'Justine' that he described it as 'the most abominable book ever engendered by the most depraved imagination.' He ordered the arrest of de Sade who spent the last thirteen years of his life in prison.

Embraces are cominglings from the head even to the feet, and not a pompous high priest entering by a secret place.

– William Blake (1757-1827). *Jerusalem, The Emanation of the Giant Albion* (1804 – 1820, with additions made even later). This poem forms the last of Blake's *Prophetic Books*. Blake held a theory of 'biological liberalism' in which no part of the body has a right to exalt itself at the expense of another – including the male 'pompous High Priest.'

Sex contains all, bodies, souls,
Meanings, proofs, purities, delicacies, results, promulgations,
All hopes, benefactions, bestowals, all the passions, loves, beauties, delights of the earth,
All the governments, judges, gods.

– Walt Whitman (1819-1892), 'A Woman Waits for Me' from *Leaves of Grass* (1860). Whitman
was part of the transition between the transcendentalism of Thoreau, Emerson and Muir, and the
realism of later American writers such as William Dean Howells and Stephen Crane. Today,
he is celebrated as one of the most influential poets in the American canon and the father of
'free verse.'

I must say that he was a very handsome man, but for his monkish vestments. The brown serge gown he wore, open in front, and merely fastened by a girdle, was not a becoming costume. What seemed strange to me was that he wore no breeches, or undergarments of any description. But I soon found out that this was intentional. Turning around, and regarding with lustful complacency the lovely posteriors and perfect charms displayed by the kneeling girl, Father Eustace briefly asked the Abbess if she had confessed her sin and promised repentance. Being answered in the affirmative, he remarked he would not use the whip but would merely administer a few gentle slaps, then whisper forgiveness, pour in a little holy oil, and the younger sister might consider herself absolved and purified. Nothing could be milder in the way of penance than this, and to my astonishment, Emilie absolutely appeared to like the gentle slapping. Instead of shrinking from it, she stuck her naked rump upwards and outwards as if to meet the infliction.

– Anonymous ('Written by a Young Nobleman'), *The Nunnery Tales,* printed and sold by the Booksellers of London and Westminster (1866); a classic Victorian erotic novel.

Sex: a sweet poison only to the withered, but to the lion-willed the great cordial and the reverently reserved wine of wines.

– Friedrich Nietzsche (1844-1900), *Thus Spoke Zarathustra: A Book for All and None* (1883-1885), which deals with ideals such as the 'eternal recurrence of the same', the parable on the 'death of God' and the 'prophecy' of the 'Übermensch.'

Bondage And Service – that was what they all demanded and from everyone. This craving to find themselves in another, to subjugate and appropriate foreign territory, to create a new field for their own will in a second body, foreign flesh for their own soul; this greedy, consuming hunger devoured every other desire, and they called it friendship!

– Hermann Bahr (1863-1934), *The School of Love* (1890); an Austrian writer, playwright, critic and active member of the Austrian avant-garde.

I regard sex as the central problem of life. And now that the problem of religion has practically been settled, and that the problem of labour has at least been placed on a practical foundation, the question of sex—with the racial questions that rest on it—stands before the coming generations as the chief problem for solution. Sex lies at the root of life, and we can never learn to reverence life until we know how to understand sex.

– Henry Havelock Ellis (1859-1939), *Studies in the Psychology of Sex* (1897). Havelock Ellis was a British physician, writer and social reformer, who co-authored the first English-language medical textbook on homosexuality.

Everything in the world is about sex except sex. Sex is about power.

I have no objection to anyone's sex life as long as they don't practice it in the street and frighten the horses.

– Oscar Wilde (1854-1900), who after his imprisonment for 'gross indecency' and early death, became a gay icon and symbol of societal repression in the latter half of the twentieth century.

THE
TWENTIETH
CENTURY

Man has imagined a heaven, and has left entirely out of it the supremest of all his delights...sexual intercourse!

His heaven is like himself: strange, interesting, astonishing, grotesque. I give you my word, it has not a single feature in it that he actually values.

– Samuel Langhorne Clemens, better known by his pen name Mark Twain (1835-1910); author of *Huckleberry Finn*, the 'Great American Novel.'

Sex is difficult; yes. But those tasks that have been entrusted to us are difficult; almost everything serious is difficult; and everything is serious. If you just recognize this and manage, out of yourself, out of your own talent and nature, out of your own experience and childhood and strength, to achieve a wholly individual relation to sex (one that is not influenced by convention and custom), then you will no longer have to be afraid of losing yourself and becoming unworthy of your dearest possession.

– Rainer Maria Rilke (1875-1926), letter from 16th July, 1903, in, *Letters to a Young Poet*.
A Bohemian-Austrian poet and novelist, Rilke's work is intense and mystical, often depicting the difficulty of communing with the natural world in the modern, cynical age.

We are to play the game of death to-night, my bride and I.
The night is black, the clouds in the sky are capricious, and
the waves are raving at the sea.

We have left our bed of dreams, flung open the door and
come out, my bride and I.

We sit upon a swing, and the storm winds give us a wild
push from behind.

My bride starts up with fear and delight, she trembles and
clings to my breast.

Long have I served her tenderly.

I made for her a bed of flowers and I closed the doors to
shut out the rude light from her eyes.

I kissed her gently on her lips and whispered softly in her

ears till she half swooned with langour.

She was lost in the endless mist of vague sweetness.

She answered not to my touch, my songs failed to arouse her.

To-night has come to us the call of the storm from the wild.

My bride has shivered and stood up, she has clasped my

hand and come out.

Her hair is flying in the wind, her veil is fluttering, her

garland rustles over her breast.

The push of death has swung her into life.

We are face to face and heart to heart, my bride and I.

– Rabindranath Tagore (1861-1941), *The Gardener* (1915). Tagore is considered one of the greatest writers in modern Indian literature – a Bengali poet, novelist and teacher who won the Nobel Prize for Literature in 1913.

Sexual love is undoubtedly one of the chief things in life, and the union of mental and bodily satisfaction in the enjoyment of love is one of its culminating peaks. Apart from a few queer fanatics, all the world knows this and conducts its life accordingly; science alone is too delicate to admit it.

Observations on Transference-Love (1915)

It is my belief that, however strange it may sound, we must reckon with the possibility that something in the nature of the sexual instinct itself is unfavourable to the realization of complete satisfaction.

On the Universal Tendency to Debasement in the Sphere of Love (1922)

– Sigmund Freud (1856-1939). Elsewhere, Freud elaborates that whilst the love instinct (eros) can be commandeered by society to bind its members together, there is also an aggressive instinct which must be either repressed or directed against a rival culture.

Of all sexual aberrations, chastity is the strangest.

– Remy de Gourmont (1858-1915), *The Natural Philosophy of Love* (1922). Gourmant
was a French Symbolist poet, novelist and influential critic.

Intercourse with a woman is sometimes a satisfactory substitute for masturbation. But it takes a lot of imagination to make it work.

– Karl Kraus (1874-1936); an Austrian writer, journalist and aphorist – famed for his satire of the German press, culture and politics.

I am still of the opinion that only two topics can be of the least interest to a serious and studious mood – sex and the dead.

– William Butler Yeats (1865-1939) – one of the foremost figures of twentieth century literature, and the first Irishman to be awarded the Nobel Prize in Literature (in 1923).

*It is sex. How wonderful sex can be,
when men keep it powerful and sacred,
and it fills the world! Like sunshine
through and through one!*

– D.H. Lawrence (1885-1930), *The Plumed Serpent* (1926), a short story published two
years before Lawrence's infamous *Lady Chatterley's Lover.*

Thus the senses are constantly being roused by the imagination. *Sex appeal is the keynote of our civilisation.* Here again, science has something to say, and it will say it one day so clearly that all must listen: there will no longer be pleasure in so much love of pleasure.

– Henri Bergson (1859-1941), *Two Sources of Morality and Religion* (1932). Bergson was one of the most influential philosophers of the twentieth century, and won the Nobel Prize in Literature in 1937.

I HAVE DONE WHAT I PLEASED, SO THAT EVERY BIT OF SEXUAL IMPULSE IN ME HAS EXPRESSED ITSELF.

– H.G. Wells (1866-1946), the father of science fiction and author of *The War of the Worlds*, *The Invisible Man* and *The Island of Doctor Moreau*.

RELIGION
ON SEX

If one, longing for sexual pleasure, achieves it, yes, he's enraptured at heart. The mortal gets what he wants. But if for that person — longing, desiring — the pleasures diminish, he's shattered, as if shot with an arrow.

So one, always mindful, should avoid sexual desires. Letting them go, he will cross over the flood like one who, having bailed out the boat, has reached the far shore.

– The teachings of Buddha, in the *Kama Sutta* (the first of the three divisions of the Pali Canon). Buddha is believed to have lived and taught mostly in eastern India sometime between the sixth and fourth centuries BCE. These words come from the *Sutta Nipata,* one of more than 10,000 suttas (teachings) attributed to Buddha or his close companions.

Therefore a man shall leave his father and his mother and hold fast to his wife, and they shall become one flesh.

– The Bible, Genesis 2:24; espousing the principle of matrimonial fidelity and sexual union – and the inherent holiness of such acts. The union between husband and wife is understood to be so strong that they become one person, one soul and one body.

There she lusted after her lovers, whose genitals were like those of donkeys and whose emission like that of horses. So you longed for the lewdness of your youth, when in Egypt your bosom was caressed and your young breasts fondled.

– The Bible, Ezekiel 23:20-21. This passage comes in the context of *the adultery of Oholah and Aholibah.*

Let the husband render to [his] wife her due; but let the wife also do likewise to [her] husband. The wife does not exercise authority over her own body, but her husband does; likewise, also, the husband does not exercise authority over his own body, but his wife does. Do not be depriving each other [of it], except by mutual consent for an appointed time...

– The Bible, Corinthians 7:3. 'Her Due' has been variously understood to mean sexual union, love, tenderness, humanity, care and protection – and the passage warns against over scrupulous asceticism which, at the time, had gained precedence amongst many believers.

It has been made permissible for you the night preceding fasting to go to your wives [for sexual relations]. They are clothing for you and you are clothing for them. Allah knows that you used to deceive yourselves, so He accepted your repentance and forgave you. So now, have relations with them and seek that which Allah has decreed for you. And eat and drink until the white thread of dawn becomes distinct to you from the black thread [of night].

– *The Quran*, Surat Al-Baqarah, 2:187. Within the Quran, marriage is continuously stressed as the only way for men and women to form a relationship where sexual activity can take place.

For those who swear not to have sexual relations with their wives is a waiting time of four months, but if they return [to normal relations] – then indeed, Allah is Forgiving and Merciful.

– *The Quran*, Surat Al-Baqarah, 2:226.

And they who guard their chastity, except from their wives or those their right hands possess, for indeed, they will not be blamed – But whoever seeks beyond that, then those are the transgressors.

– *The Quran*, Surat Al-Mu'minn, 23:5-7. The meaning of 'those who their right hands possess' has been heavily debated, however many scholars take it to mean that it is permissible for a man to have sex with his (female) slaves, as well as his wife.

Once you see your nature, sex is basically immaterial.

– Bodhidharma, a Buddhist monk who lived during the fifth or sixth century CE. He is traditionally credited as the transmitter of Ch'an (Zen) to China, and is regarded as its first Chinese patriarch.

Because every portion of the body, mind, and spirit yearns for the integration of yin and yang, angelic intercourse is led by the spirit rather than the sexual organs. . . . Where ordinary intercourse unites sex organs with sex organs, angelic cultivation unites spirit with spirit, mind with mind, and every cell of one body with every cell of the other body.

– Lao-Tzu (usually dated to around the sixth century BCE), was a philosopher and a poet of ancient China, best known as the reputed author of the *Tao Te Ching* and the founder of philosophical Taoism. Lao-Tzu is also revered as a deity in religious Taoism and many traditional Chinese religions, which emphasise living in harmony with the *Tao* (meaning 'path' or 'principle' – something that is both the source and driving force behind everything that exists).

A man should gather from the actions of the woman of what disposition she is, and in what way she likes to be enjoyed.

Whatever things may be done by one of the lovers to the other, the same should be returned by the other.

In short, nothing tends to increase love so much as the effects of marking with the nails, and biting.

As variety is necessary in love, so love is to be produced by means of variety.

– The *Kama Sutra*, an ancient Indian Hindu text widely considered to be the standard work on human sexual behaviour. It was written sometime between 400 BCE and 200 CE, and contrary to popular perception, is not just a sex manual, but presents itself as a guide to a virtuous and gracious living. 'Kama' which is one of the four goals of Hindu life, means desire – including sexual desire, the latter being the subject of the textbook, and 'sutra' literally means a thread or line that holds things together.

One should know that sexual union is holy and pure when it is done as it should be, at the time it should be, and with proper intent.

– From the the *Iggeret HaKodesh* (*The Holy Letter*), a thirteenth century treatise on sexuality, most often ascribed to Nahmanides, also known as Rabbi Moshe ben Nahman Girondi (1194-1270), a leading medieval Jewish scholar. The first commandment in the Torah is 'Be fruitful and multiply', and procreation is one of the reasons that sex is considered holy.

The way you make love
is the way God will be with you.

– Rumi (also known as Jall ad-Dn Muhammad Rm), *The Book of Love*. Rumi (1207-1273) was a Persian poet, jurist, theologian and Sufi mystic, whose importance is considered to transcend national and ethnic borders. Sufism is a concept in Islam, defined by scholars as the inner, mystical dimension of the religion.

Natural inclinations are present in things from God, who moves all things. So it is impossible for the natural inclinations of a species to be toward evil in itself. But there is in all perfect animals a natural inclination toward carnal union. Therefore it is impossible for carnal union to be evil in itself.

– Thomas Aquinas (1225-1274), an Italian Dominican friar and priest – and an immensely influential philosopher and theologian. This passage comes from the *Summa Contra Gentiles* (*c.*1260-1264), one of Aquinas's best known works.

HE WHO LOVES NOT WOMEN, WINE AND SONG REMAINS A FOOL HIS WHOLE LIFE LONG

– Martin Luther (1483-1546), a German friar and father of the Protestant Reformation who protested against the Catholic theology of indulgences (what he saw as the purchase and sale of salvation).

Marital intercourse is certainly holy, lawful and praiseworthy in itself and profitable to society, yet in certain circumstances it can prove dangerous, as when through excess the soul is made sick with venial sin, or through the violation and perversion of its primary end, killed by mortal sin; such perversion, detestable in proportion to its departure from the true order, being always mortal sin, for it is never lawful to exclude the primary end of marriage which is the procreation of children.

– Francis de Sales (1567-1622), the Bishop of Geneva honoured as a Saint in the Roman Catholic Church. He became noted for his deep faith and gentle approach to the religious divisions in his land resulting from the Protestant Reformation.

Renounce sexual desire, anger, falsehood and slander; forsake maya and eliminate egotistical pride. Renounce lust and promiscuity, and give up emotional attachment. Only then shall you obtain the Immaculate Lord amidst the darkness of the world.

– Guru Granth Sahib Ji,141-13; the central religious text of Sikhism, a voluminous work of 1430 *Angs* (pages), compiled and composed during the period of Sikh gurus, from 1469 to 1708. 'Maya' literally translates as 'delusion' but can also refer to wealth, illusion and transitory qualities.

It is the duty of every thoughtful Indian not to marry. In case he is helpless in regard to marriage, he should abstain from sexual intercourse with his wife.

– Mahatma Gandhi (1869-1948); the pre-eminent leader of Indian nationalism in British ruled India, who inspired movements for civil rights and freedom across the world. Ghandi's vision was for a free India based on religious pluralism, and his non-violent civil disobedience was largely inspired by the Hindu teachings of love and equality.

BANNED BOOKS

Now it so befell that after a hard day's work he was taking a little rest, when two young nuns, who were walking in the garden, approached the spot where he lay, and stopped to look at him, while he pretended to be asleep. And so the bolder of the two said to the other: 'If I thought thou wouldst keep the secret, I would tell thee what I have sometimes meditated, and which thou perhaps mightest also find agreeable'.... So she took him by the hand with a blandishing air, to which he replied with some clownish grins. And then she led him into the hut, where he needed no pressing to do what she desired of him. Which done, she changed places with the other, as loyal comradeship required; and Masetto, still keeping up the pretence of simplicity, did their pleasure.

– Giovanni Boccaccio (1313-1375), *The Decameron* (1350-1353). This masterpiece of Italian literature depicts 100 tales told by seven young women and three young men, ranging from the erotic to the tragic, and comedy to moralising. It was banned in America under the Federal Anti-Obscenity Act of 1873, which prohibited the sending or receiving of works containing 'obscene', 'filthy' or 'inappropriate' material.

Old English	Modern English
The wyndow she undoth, and that in haste.	The window she unbarred, and that in haste.
Have do, quod she, com of, and speed the faste,	'Have done,' said she, 'come on, and do it fast,
Lest that oure neighebores thee espie.	Before we're seen by any neighbour's eye.'
This absolon gan wype his mouth ful drie.	This Absalom did wipe his mouth all dry;
Derk was the nyght as pich, or as the cole,	Dark was the night as pitch, aye dark as coal,
And at the wyndow out she putte hir hole,	And through the window she put out her hole.
And absolon, hym fil no bet ne wers,	And Absalom no better felt nor worse,
But with his mouth he kiste hir naked ers	But with his mouth he kissed her naked arse
Ful savourly, er he were war of this.	Right greedily, before he knew of this.
Abak he stirte, and thoughte it was amys,	Aback he leapt– it seemed somehow amiss,
For wel he wiste a womman hath no berd.	For well he knew a woman has no beard;
He felte a thyng al rough and long yherd,	He'd felt a thing all rough and longish haired,
And seyde, fy! allas! what have I do?	And said, 'Oh fie, alas! What did I do?'
Tehee! quod she, and clapte the wyndow to...	'Teehee!' she laughed, and clapped the, window to...

– Geoffrey Chaucer (1343-1400), 'The Miller's Tale' from *The Canterbury Tales* (1380s-1390s). The risqué extract above forms part of a story told by the drunken miller Robyn, to repay 'The Knight's Tale.' Like the *Decameron,* it was banned from U.S. mail under the Federal Anti-Obscenity Act.

As for me, my business was his money, and what I could make of him; and after that, if I could have found out any way to have done it, I would have sent him safe home to his house and to his family, for 'twas ten to one but he had an honest, virtuous wife and innocent children, that were anxious for his safety, and would have been glad to have gotten him home, and have taken care of him till he was restored to himself. And then with what shame and regret would he look back upon himself! how would he reproach himself with associating himself with a whore! picked up in the worst of all holes, the cloister, among the dirt and filth of all the town! how would he be trembling for fear he had got the pox, for fear a dart had struck through his liver, and hate himself every time he looked back upon the madness and brutality of his debauch!

– Daniel Defoe (1660-1731), *The Fortunes and Misfortunes of the Famous Moll Flanders* (1722). Defoe was a noted social reformer, especially concerned with prison and asylum conditions. *Moll Flanders* purports to be the true account of the life of the eponymous Moll, detailing her exploits from birth until old age. For its depictions of prostitution, it was also banned under the U.S Federal Anti-Obscenity Act.

One day Cunegonde, while walking near the castle, in a little wood which they called a park, saw between the bushes, Dr. Pangloss giving a lesson in experimental natural philosophy to her mother's chamber-maid, a little brown wench, very pretty and very docile. As Miss Cunegonde had a great disposition for the sciences, she breathlessly observed the repeated experiments of which she was a witness; she clearly perceived the force of the Doctor's reasons, the effects, and the causes; she turned back greatly flurried, quite pensive, and filled with the desire to be learned; dreaming that she might well be a *sufficient reason* for young Candide, and he for her.

– Voltaire (1694-1778), *Candide* (1759). Immediately after publication, the work and its author were denounced by both secular and religious authorities and by the end of February 1759, the Grand Council of Geneva banned the novel. *Candide* nevertheless succeeded in selling twenty thousand to thirty thousand copies by the end of the year in over twenty editions, making it a best seller. In 1762, *Candide* was listed in the *Index Librorum Prohibitorum*, the Roman Catholic Church's list of prohibited books. It was further seized by U.S Customs in 1929, for its 'obscene nature.'

I lay then all tame and passive as she could wish, whilst her freedom raised no other emotion but those of a strange, and, till then, unfelt pleasure. Every part of me was open and exposed to the licentious courses of her hands, which, like a lambent fire, ran over my whole body, and thawed all coldness as they went.

My breasts, if it is not too bold a figure to call so two hard, firm, rising hillocks, that just began to shew themselves, or signify anything to the touch, employed and amused her hands awhile, till, slipping down lower, over a smooth track, she could just feel the soft silky down that had but a few months before put forth and garnished the mount-pleasant of those parts, and promised to spread a grateful shelter over the sweet seat of the most exquisite sensation, and which had been, till that instant, the seat of the most insensible innocence. Her fingers played and strove to twine in the young tendrils of that moss, which nature has contrived at once for use and ornament.

But, not contented with these outer posts, she now attempts the main spot, and began to twitch, to insinuate, and at length to force an introduction of a finger into the quick itself, in such a manner, that had she not proceeded by insensible gradations that inflamed me beyond the power of modesty to oppose its resistance to their progress, I should have jumped out of bed and cried for help against such strange assaults.... the extension of my limbs, languid stretching, sighs, short heavings, all conspired to assure that experienced wanton that I was more pleased than offended at her proceedings, which she seasoned with repeated kisses and exclamations, such as 'Oh! what a charming creature thou art! What a happy man will he be that first makes a woman of you! Oh! that I were a man for your sake!' with the like broken expressions, interrupted by kisses as fierce and salacious as ever I received from the other sex.

For my part, I was transported, confused, and out of myself; feelings so new were too much for me. My heated and alarmed senses were in a tumult that robbed me of all liberty of thought; tears of pleasure gushed from my eyes, and somewhat assuaged the fire that raged all over me.

– John Cleland (1709-1789), *Memoirs of a Woman of Pleasure* (popularly known as *Fanny Hill*), first published in 1748 – considered to be 'the first original English prose pornography, and the first pornography to use the form of the novel.' The book's depictions of homosexuality caused considerable outrage in eighteenth century Britain. It is one of the most prosecuted books in history and was not published (legally) in its full form in the U.K until 1970.

Smiling a strange smile, his pupil fixed, his teeth set, he advanced with outstretched arms. She recoiled trembling. She stammered: 'Oh, you frighten me! You hurt me! Let me go!'

'If it must be,' he went on, his face changing; and he again became respectful, caressing, timid.

She gave him her arm. They went back. He said: 'What was the matter with you? Why? I do not understand. You were mistaken, no doubt. In my soul you are as a Madonna on a pedestal, in a place lofty, secure, immaculate. But I need you to live! I must have your eyes, your voice, your thought! Be my friend, my sister, my angel!'

And he put out his arm round her waist. She feebly tried to disengage herself. He supported her thus as they walked along. But they heard the two horses browsing on the leaves.

'Oh! one moment!' said Rodolphe. 'Do not let us go! Stay!'

He drew her farther on to a small pool where duckweeds made a greenness on the water. Faded water lilies lay motionless between the reeds. At the noise of their steps in the grass, frogs jumped away to hide themselves.

'I am wrong! I am wrong!' she said. 'I am mad to listen to you!'

'Why? Emma! Emma!'

'Oh, Rodolphe!' said the young woman slowly, leaning on his shoulder.

The cloth of her habit caught against the velvet of his coat. She threw back her white neck, swelling with a sigh, and faltering, in tears, with a long shudder and hiding her face, she gave herself up to him.

– Gustave Flaubert (1821-1880), *Madame Bovary* (1856); the story of a doctor's wife who has adulterous affairs in order to escape the banalities of provincial life. When it was first serialised in *La Revue de Paris* between 1st October and 15th December 1856, the novel was attacked for obscenity by public prosecutors. It was temporarily banned for 'offences against public morals' though Flaubert was acquitted one year later.

And she saw a long Roman candle going up over the trees, up, up, and, in the tense hush, they were all breathless with excitement as it went higher and higher and she had to lean back more and more to look up after it, high, high, almost out of sight, and her face was suffused with a divine, an entrancing blush from straining back and he could see her other things too, nainsook knickers, the fabric that caresses the skin, better than those other pettiwidth, the green, four and eleven, on account of being white and she let him and she saw that he saw and then it went so high it went out of sight a moment and she was trembling in every limb from being bent so far back that he had a full view high up above her knee where no-one ever not even on the swing or wading and she wasn't ashamed and he wasn't either to look in that immodest way like that because he couldn't resist the sight of the wondrous revealment half offered like those skirtdancers behaving so immodest before gentlemen looking and he kept on looking, looking. She would fain have cried to him chokingly, held out her snowy slender arms to him to come, to feel his lips laid on her white brow, the cry of a young girl's love, a little strangled cry, wrung from her, that cry that has rung through the ages. And then a rocket sprang and bang shot blind blank and O! then the Roman candle burst and it was like a sigh of O! and everyone cried O! O! in raptures and it gushed out of it a stream of rain gold hair threads and they shed and ah! they were all greeny dewy stars falling with golden, O so lovely, O, soft, sweet, soft!

– James Joyce (1882-1941), *Ulysses* (1922). This extract, the 'Nausicaa Episode', led to the book's prosecution for obscenity. It was banned in the U.K until the 1930s, and challenged and temporarily banned in the U.S for its sexual content. Throughout the 1920s, the United States Post Office Department burned copies of the novel. The American prohibition was overturned in 1933 with the famous case of 'United States versus One Book Called Ulysses.'

And when he came into her, with an intensification of relief and consummation that was pure peace to him, still she was waiting. She felt herself a little left out. And she knew, partly it was her own fault. She willed herself into this separateness. Now perhaps she was condemned to it. She lay still, feeling his motion within her, his deep-sunk intentness, the sudden quiver of him at the springing of his seed, then the slow-subsiding thrust. That thrust of the buttocks, surely it was a little ridiculous. If you were a woman, and a part in all the business, surely that thrusting of the man's buttocks was supremely ridiculous. Surely the man was intensely ridiculous in this posture and this act...Yes, this was love, this ridiculous bouncing of the buttocks, and the wilting of the poor, insignificant, moist little penis. This was the divine love!!

– D.H. Lawrence (1885-1930), *Lady Chatterley's Lover* (1928). The book quickly became notorious for its story of the physical (and emotional) relationship between a working-class man and an upper-class woman, its explicit descriptions of sex, and its use of then-unprintable words. It was banned in the U.S and the U.K for violation of obscenity laws, but both interdictions were lifted in 1959 and 1960 respectively. It was also banned in Australia from 1929 to 1965.

Oh, but now she must pay to the uttermost farthing for the madness that had left those words unspoken–even as her father had paid before her. With Mary's kisses still hot on her lips, she must pay and pay unto the uttermost farthing. And because of an anguish that seemed past endurance, she spoke roughly; the words when they came were cruel. She spared neither the girl who must listen to them, nor herself who must force her to stand there and listen.

'Have you understood? Do you realize now what it's going to mean if you give yourself to me?' Then she stopped abruptly...Mary was crying.

Stephen said, and her voice had grown quite toneless: 'It's too much to ask–you're right; it's too much. I had to tell you–forgive me, Mary.'

But Mary turned on her with very bright eyes: 'You can say that–you, who talk about loving! What do I care for all you've told me? What do I care for the world's opinion? What do I care for anything but you, and you just as you are–as you are, I love you! Do you think I'm crying because of what you've told me? I'm crying because of your dear, scarred face...the misery on it...Can't you understand that all that I am belongs to you, Stephen?'

Stephen bent down and kissed Mary's hands very humbly, for now she could find no words any more...and that night they were not divided.

– Radclyffe Hall (1880-1943), *The Well of Loneliness* (1928), a novel following the 'sexual inversions' of its lesbian protagonist, Stephen Gordon. The novel became the target of a campaign by James Douglas, editor of the *Sunday Express* newspaper, who wrote, 'I would rather give a healthy boy or a healthy girl a phial of prussic acid than this novel.' Although its only sexual reference consists of the words 'and that night, they were not divided', a British court judged it obscene because it defended 'unnatural practices between women.' It was republished in 1949.

SEX
LETTERS

21st November 1796

I am going to bed with my heart full of your adorable image... I cannot wait to give you proofs of my ardent love... How happy I would be if I could assist you at your undressing, the little firm white breast, the adorable face, the hair tied up in a scarf a la creole. You know that I will never forget the little visits, you know, the little black forest... I kiss it a thousand times and wait impatiently for the moment I will be in it. To live within Joséphine is to live in the Elysian fields. Kisses on your mouth, your eyes, your breast, everywhere, everywhere.

November 1796

I don't love you anymore; on the contrary, I detest you. You are a vile, mean, beastly slut. You don't write to me at all; you don't love your husband; you know how happy your letters make him, and you don't write him six lines of nonsense...

Soon, I hope, I will be holding you in my arms; then I will cover you with a million hot kisses, burning like the equator.

– Napoleon Bonaparte to Joséphine de Beauharnais, written during his campaigns in Italy of 1797. Her beauty was infamous, and after their meeting in 1795, Bonaparte was infatuated. They married in 1796 (despite social disapproval, as Joséphine was a widowed mother of two), but in the same year she began an affair with a handsome Hussar lieutenant Hippolyte Charles – rumours of which infuriated Bonaparte. Six days after writing the first letter, he returned to her apartment in Milan, to find it empty. Suspecting she was with Charles, Napoleon's love turned to jealousy.

My beloved angel,

I am nearly mad about you, as much as one can be mad: I cannot bring together two ideas that you do not interpose yourself between them. I can no longer think of nothing but you. In spite of myself, my imagination carries me to you. I grasp you, I kiss you, I caress you, a thousand of the most amorous caresses take possession of me.

– Honoré de Balzac to Ewelina Haska in June 1835. The two had a passionate affair, and intensely corresponded. Haska promised to marry Balzac on the death of her husband, but her family prevented this pairing by threatening to contest Haska's inheritance. Fearful she and her daughter would be left destitute, Haska wrote to Balzac in 1841 stating simply 'You are free.' The couple eventually married in March of 1850, but Balzac died just four months after the wedding, leaving Haska distraught.

I will cover you with love when next I see you, with caresses,

with ecstasy. I want to gorge you with all the joys of the flesh,

so that you faint and die. I want you to be amazed by me,

and to confess to yourself that you had never even dreamed of

such transports… When you are old, I want you to recall those

few hours, I want your dry bones to quiver with joy when you

think of them.

– Gustave Flaubert (1821-1880), writing to Louise Colet in 1846. His affair with Colet was
Flaubert's only serious romantic relationship, although he never married.

Songs of longing!

And they will resound in my letters, just as they always have, sometimes loudly and sometimes secretly so that you alone can hear them... But they will also be different — different from how they used to be, these songs. For I have turned and found longing at my side, and I have looked into her eyes, and now she leads me with a steady hand.

– Rainer Maria Rilke (1875-1926) writing to his lover, Lou Andreas-Solomé on 3rd June 1897. Despite near constant rejections from the married Solomé, Rilke persevered and the two went on to have a thirty-five year long relationship.

My Own Boy,

Your sonnet is quite lovely, and it is a marvel that those red rose-leaf lips of yours should be made no less for the madness of music and song than for the madness of kissing. Your slim gilt soul walks between passion and poetry. I know Hyacinthus, whom Apollo loved so madly, was you in Greek days. [...]

Always, with undying love, yours,

Oscar

– Oscar Wilde to Lord Alfred 'Bosie' Douglas. Wilde met Douglas in June of 1891 and the young man became Wilde's muse, confidant and lover. Wilde, who was earning up to £100 a week from his plays, indulged Douglas's every whim: material, artistic or sexual. By 1893 Wilde was infatuated with Douglas and they consorted together regularly in a tempestuous affair – which eventually led to Wilde's trial for 'gross indecency with other men', subsequent conviction to two year's hard labour, and final self-exile to France.

There would have been the making of
an accomplished flirt in me, because my
lucidity shows me each move of the game
– but that, in the same instant, a reaction of
contempt makes me sweep all the counters
off the board and cry out: – 'Take them
all – I don't want to win – I want to lose
everything to you!'

– Edith Wharton (1862-1937), writing to W. Morton Fullerton in 1908. Her husband
(Edward Wharton) was deemed to be of an 'incurable mental state' in 1908, and the
couple divorced in 1913. Around the same time, Edith started an affair with Fullerton, a
journalist for the *Times;* both a romantic and intellectual partner.

My sweet little whorish Nora I did as you told me, you dirty little girl, and pulled myself off twice when I read your letter. I am delighted to see that you do like being fucked arseways. Yes, now I can remember that night when I fucked you for so long backwards. It was the dirtiest fucking I ever gave you, darling. My prick was stuck in you for hours, fucking in and out under your upturned rump. I felt your fat sweaty buttocks under my belly and saw your flushed face and mad eyes. At every fuck I gave you your shameless tongue came bursting out through your lips and if a gave you a bigger stronger fuck than usual, fat dirty farts came spluttering out of your backside. You had an arse full of farts that night, darling, and I fucked them out of you, big fat fellows, long windy ones, quick little merry cracks and a lot of tiny little naughty farties ending in a long gush from your hole. It is wonderful to fuck a farting woman when every fuck drives one out of her. I think I would know Nora's fart anywhere. I think I could pick hers out in a roomful of farting women. It is a rather girlish noise not like the wet windy fart which I imagine fat wives have. It is sudden and dry and dirty like what a bold girl would let off in fun in a school dormitory at night. I hope Nora will let off no end of her farts in my face so that I may know their smell also...

Goodnight, my little farting Nora, my dirty little fuckbird! There is one lovely word, darling, you have underlined to make me pull myself off better. Write me more about that and yourself, sweetly, dirtier, dirtier.

– James Joyce (1882-1941), considered to be one of the most influential writers of the twentieth century, famed for *Ulysses* (1922) and *Dubliners* (1914). The above is an excerpt from a letter to his wife, Nora Barnacle on 8th December 1909.

Last night I dreamed about you. What happened in detail I can hardly remember, all I know is that we kept merging into one another. I was you, you were me. Finally you somehow caught fire.

Remembering that one extinguished fire with clothing, I took an old coat and beat you with it.

But again the transmutations began and it went so far that you were no longer even there, instead it was I who was on fire and it was also I who beat the fire with the coat.

But the beating didn't help and it only confirmed my old fear that such things can't extinguish a fire.

In the meantime, however, the fire brigade arrived and somehow you were saved.

But you were different from before, spectral, as though drawn with chalk against the dark, and you fell, lifeless or perhaps having fainted from joy at having been saved, into my arms.

But here too the uncertainty of trans mutability entered, perhaps it was I who fell into someone's arms.

– Franz Kafka (1883-1924) writing to Milen Jesenská in 1921. This classically Kafka-esque love letter, was written one year after he began an intense relationship with Jesenská, a Czech journalist and writer.

FORBIDDEN LUST

Abstain from censure; for it will strengthen the censured,

and increase desire into violent passion. If I suffer such

passion, my case is but the same as that of many a man before

me: For greatly indeed to be wondered at is he who hath kept

himself safe from women's artifice.

– *One Thousand and One Nights,* a collection of West and South Asian stories complied
during the Islamic Golden Age (*c.* 622-1258). It is known in English as the *Arabian
Nights* from the first edition of 1706, converted from Antoine Galland's French translation
of 1704.

LOVE CEASES TO BE A PLEASURE WHEN IT CEASES TO BE A SECRET.

– Aphra Behn (1640-1689), *The Lover's Watch,* 'Four o'clock General Conversation' (1686). A prolific dramatist of the English Restoration, Behn was one of the first English professional female writers. Along with Delarivier Manley and Eliza Haywood, she is referred to as part of 'The fair triumvirate of wit.'

Who would believe this childish discipline, received at eight-years old, from the hands of a woman of 30, should influence my propensities, my desires, my passions, for the rest of my life, and that in quite a contrary sense from what might naturally have been expected? The very incident that inflamed my senses, gave my desires such an extraordinary turn, that, confined to what I had already experienced, I sought no further, and, with blood boiling with sensuality, almost from my birth, preserved my purity beyond the age when the coldest constitutions lose their insensibility...

– Jean Jacques Rousseau (1712-1778), whose political philosophy inspired the French Revolution. Here, in *The Confessions of J.J. Rousseau* (posthumously published in 1782), he alludes to his love of spanking and subsequent sexual denial.

I shall possess this woman; I shall steal her from the husband who profanes her: I will even dare ravish her from the God whom she adores. What delight, to be in turns the object and the victor of her remorse! Far be it from me to destroy the prejudices which sway her mind! They will add to my happiness and my triumph. Let her believe in virtue, and sacrifice it to me; let the idea of falling terrify her, without preventing her fall; and may she, shaken by a thousand terrors, forget them, vanquish them only in my arms.

– Pierre Choderlos de Laclos (1741-1803), *Dangerous Liaisons* (1782); a French epistolary novel depicting the story of two rivals (and ex-lovers) who use seduction as a weapon to humiliate and degrade others, all the while enjoying their cruel games and boasting about their manipulative talents.

When once the woman has tempted us, and we have tasted the forbidden fruit, there is no such thing as checking our appetites, whatever the consequences may be.

– George Washington (1731-1799), the first President of the United States – writing a letter to Mrs. Richard Stockton on 2nd September 1783.

Ye jovial boys who love the joys.
The blissful joys of Lovers;
Yet dare avow with dauntless brow,
When th' bony lass discovers;
Pray draw near and lend an ear,
And welcome in a Prater,
For I've lately been on quarantine,
A proven Fornicator.
Before the Congregation wide
I pass'd the muster fairly,
My handsome Betsey by my side,
We gat our ditty rarely;

But my downcast eye by chance did spy
What made my lips to water,
Those limbs so clean where I, between,
Commenc'd a Fornicator.
With rueful face and signs of grace
I pay'd the buttock-hire,
The night was dark and thro' the park
I could not but convoy her;
A parting kiss, what could I less,
My vows began to scatter,
My Betsey fell-lal de dal lal lal,
I am a Fornicator.

– Robert Burns (1759-1796), 'The Fornicator' (1785), this bawdy song refers to Burns's
censure by the church for his affair with a servant girl, Elizabeth Patten – and further, his
refusal to take the punishment seriously. He is instead distracted by the bare legs of his
'handsome Betsey.'

If it is the dirty element that gives pleasure to the act of lust, then the dirtier it is, the more pleasurable it is bound to be.

– Marquis de Sade (1740-1814), *120 Days of Sodom, or the School of Libertinism* (1785), which due to its depictions of sexual violence and extreme cruelty, has been banned by many countries.

And Julia's voice was lost, except in sighs,

    Until too late for useful conversation;

The tears were gushing from her gentle eyes,

    I wish, indeed, they had not had occasion;

But who, alas! can love, and then be wise?

    Not that remorse did not oppose temptation;

A little still she strove, and much repented,

And whispering 'I will ne'er consent'–consented.

– Lord Byron (1788-1824), *Don Juan,* a lengthy narrative poem based on the legend of Don Juan, which Byron reverses, portraying Juan not as a womaniser but as someone easily seduced by women. When the first two cantos were published anonymously in 1819, the poem was criticised for its 'immoral content', though it was also immensely popular.

Saturday 12 July 1823 [Halifax]

Could not sleep last night. Dozing, hot & disturbed ... a violent longing for a female companion came over me. Never remember feeling it so painfully before ... It was absolute pain to me.

– Anne Lister (1791-1840), a Yorkshire landowner, diarist, mountaineer and traveller. Throughout her life she kept diaries which chronicled the details of her daily life, including her financial concerns, industrial activities and lesbian relationships. Most of the entries concerning her romantic and sexual relationships were written in code. Called 'Fred' by her lover and 'Gentleman Jack' by Halifax residents, she suffered much harassment for her sexuality.

Through me forbidden voices,

Voices of sexes and lusts, voices veil'd and I remove the veil,

Voices indecent by me clarified and transfigur'd.

I do not press my fingers across my mouth,

I keep as delicate around the bowels as around the head and heart,

Copulation is no more rank to me than death is.

– Walt Whitman (1819-1892), 'Song of Myself' from *Leaves of Grass* (1855).

The true man wants two things;
danger and play. For that reason
he wants a woman, as the most
dangerous plaything.

– Friedrich Nietzsche (1844-1900), *Thus Spoke Zarathustra: A Book for All and None* (1883-1885).

The fair girl went on her knees, and bent over me, fairly gloating. There was a deliberate voluptuousness which was both thrilling and repulsive, and as she arched her neck she actually licked her lips like an animal, till I could see in the moonlight the moisture shining on the scarlet lips and on the red tongue as it lapped the white sharp teeth. Then she paused, and I could hear the churning sound of her tongue as it licked her teeth and lips, and could feel the hot breath on my neck. Then the skin of my throat began to tingle as one's flesh does when the hand that is to tickle it approaches nearer—nearer. I could feel the soft, shivering touch of the lips on the super-sensitive skin of my throat, and the hard dents of two sharp teeth, just touching and pausing there. I closed my eyes in a languorous ecstasy and waited—waited with beating heart.

– Bram Stoker (1847-1912), *Dracula* (1897), a Gothic horror novel and early example of the modern *vampire genre*. The vampire's 'kiss' is described in overtly sexual terms with traditional gender power-dynamics reversed.

THE FIRST TWO FACTS WHICH A HEALTHY BOY OR GIRL FEELS ABOUT SEX ARE THESE: FIRST THAT IT IS BEAUTIFUL AND THEN THAT IT IS DANGEROUS.

– Gilbert K. Chesterton (1874-1936) – often referred to as the 'prince of paradox.' Here writing in the *Illustrated London News* on 1st September 1909.

He had felt proud and happy then, happy that she was his, proud of her grace and wifely carriage. But now, after the kindling again of so many memories, the first touch of her body, musical and strange and perfumed, sent through him a keen pang of lust. Under cover of her silence he pressed her arm closely to his side; and, as they stood at the hotel door, he felt that they had escaped from their lives and duties, escaped from home and friends and run away together with wild and radiant hearts to a new adventure.

An old man was dozing in a great hooded chair in the hall. He lit a candle in the office and went before them to the stairs. They followed him in silence, their feet falling in soft thuds on the thickly carpeted stairs. She mounted the stairs behind the porter, her head bowed in the ascent, her frail shoulders curved as with a burden, her skirt girt tightly about her. He could have flung his arms about her hips and held her still, for his arms were trembling with desire to seize her and only the stress of his nails against the palms of his hands held the wild impulse of his body in check. The porter halted on the stairs to settle his guttering candle. They halted, too, on the steps below him. In the silence Gabriel could hear the falling of the molten wax into the tray and the thumping of his own heart against his ribs.

– James Joyce (1882-1941), *Dubliners* (1914). Though depicting a married couple, the scene is clandestine. Gabriel is almost overcome with lust, just before he discovers that there's a lot about his wife that he doesn't know.

ROMANTICS
VS. REALISTS

LORD, GRANT ME CHASTITY AND CONTINENCE... BUT NOT YET.

– Saint Augustine of Hippo (354–430 CE). As a youth Augustine lived a hedonistic lifestyle, associating with young men who boasted of their sexual exploits with both women and men. They urged inexperienced boys, like Augustine, to seek experience – and it was during this period that he uttered this now famous prayer.

The art of procreation and the members employed

therein are so repulsive, that if it were not for the beauty

of the faces and the adornments of the actors and the

pent-up impulse, nature would lose the human species.

– Leonardo da Vinci (1452-1519), the Italian painter, architect, mathematician, engineer, geologist and writer whose genius, perhaps more than that of any other figure, epitomized the Renaissance humanist ideal.

Is it not strange that desire should so many years outlive performance?

– William Shakespeare (1564-1616), *King Henry IV; Part II*, Act II, scene 4 (believed to be written between *c*.1596 and 1599).

Brute force or bribes of diamonds

Bend others to your will,

But gentle words have greater power

And gain more conquests still.

– Charles Perrault (1628-1703), the author of Cinderella, Sleeping Beauty and Puss in Boots, on the power of 'gentle words'; the 'Second Moral' from Perrault's Fairy Tales, first published as Tales of Mother Goose in 1697.

Sex: the pleasure is momentary, the position ridiculous, and the expense damnable.

– Philip Stanhope, 4th Earl of Chesterfield (1694-1773); a British statesman and man of letters.

In all your Amours you should prefer old Women to young ones. You call this a Paradox, and demand my Reasons. They are these:

1. Because as they have more Knowledge of the World and their Minds are better stor'd with Observations, their Conversation is more improving and more lastingly agreable.

2. Because when Women cease to be handsome, they study to be good. To maintain their Influence over Men, they supply the Diminution of Beauty by an Augmentation of Utility. They learn to do a 1000 Services small and great, and are the most tender and useful of all Friends when you are sick. Thus they continue amiable. And hence there is hardly such a thing to be found as an old Woman who is not a good Woman.

3. Because there is no hazard of Children, which irregularly produc'd may be attended with much Inconvenience.

4. Because thro' more Experience, they are more prudent and discreet in conducting an Intrigue to prevent Suspicion. The Commerce with them is therefore safer with regard to your Reputation. And with regard to theirs, if the Affair should happen to be known, considerate People might be rather inclin'd to excuse an old Woman who would kindly take care of a young Man, form his Manners by her good Counsels, and prevent his ruining his Health and Fortune among mercenary Prostitutes.

5. Because in every Animal that walks upright, the Deficiency of the Fluids that fill the Muscles appears first in the highest Part: The Face first grows lank and wrinkled; then the Neck; then the Breast and Arms; the lower Parts continuing to the last as plump as ever: So that covering all above with a Basket, and regarding only what is below the Girdle, it is impossible of two Women to know an old from a young one. And as in the dark all Cats are grey, the Pleasure of corporal Enjoyment with an old Woman is at least equal, and frequently superior, every Knack being by Practice capable of Improvement.

6. Because the Sin is less. The debauching a Virgin may be her Ruin, and make her for Life unhappy.

7. Because the Compunction is less. The having made a young Girl miserable may give you frequent bitter Reflections; none of which can attend the making an old Woman happy.

8thly and Lastly They are so grateful!!

– Benjamin Franklin (1706-1790), one of the Founding Fathers of the United States, discussing the merits of conducting affairs with older women. This advice was given in a letter on 25th June 1745 to 'a young friend on the choice of a mistress.'

FUCK! IS ONE EXPECTED TO BE A GENTLEMAN WHEN ONE IS STIFF?

– Marquis de Sade (1740-1814), the French author and libertine who gave his name to the modern terms *sadism* and *sadist*.

It is true from early habit, one must make love

mechanically as one swims; I was once very fond of

both, but now as I never swim unless I tumble into the

water, I don't make love till almost obliged.

– Lord Byron (1788-1824) writing to Lady Melbourne on 10th September 1812. The
'obliging' Byron is placed in stark similarity to his reluctant protagonist, *Don Juan*.
Nonetheless, Byron was renowned in life for his aristocratic excesses, numerous love
affairs with both sexes, and rumours of a scandalous liaison with his half-sister.

One half of the world cannot understand the pleasures of the other.

– Jane Austen (1775-1817), *Emma* (1815) – a comic novel generally regarded as the most perfectly constructed of all Austen's works, concerning the perils of misconstrued romance.

Unfelt, unheard, unseen,
I've left my little queen,
Her languid arms in silver slumber lying:
Ah! through their nestling touch,
Who — who could tell how much
There is for madness — cruel, or complying?

Those faery lids how sleek!
Those lips how moist! — they speak,
In ripest quiet, shadows of sweet sounds:
Into my fancy's ear
Melting a burden dear,
How Love doth know no fulness, and no bounds.

True — tender monitors!
I bend unto your laws:
This sweetest day for dalliance was born!
So, without more ado,
I'll feel my heaven anew,
For all the blushing of the hasty morn.

– John Keats (1795-1821), 'Unfelt, Unheard, Unseen' (1817) – one of the main
figures of the second generation of Romantic poets along with Lord Byron and Percy
Bysshe Shelley.

I lose my respect for the man who can make the mystery of sex the subject of a coarse jest, yet when you speak earnestly and seriously on the subject, is silent.

– Henry David Thoreau (1817-1862), the great American naturalist and transcendentalist, famed for his avocation of simple living. Journal entry from 12th April 1852.

The sexual impulse... appears as a malevolent demon that strives to pervert, confuse, and overthrow everything.

– Arthur Schopenhauer (1788-1860), *The Metaphysics of Sexual Love* (1859). Schopenhauer was one of the first philosophers since the days of Greek philosophy to address the subject of male homosexuality. In this third, expanded edition of *The World as Will and Representation*, Schopenhauer added an appendix to his chapter *Sexual Love*, noting that homosexuality did have the benefit of preventing ill-begotten children.

'... And no lover has ever kissed you before?'

'Never'

'I knew that; you were so unused. You ride well, but you don't kiss nicely at all.'

– Thomas Hardy (1840-1928), *A Pair of Blue Eyes* (1873), a novel drawing on Hardy's courtship of his first wife, Emma Lavinia Gifford whom he married in 1874. Although they later became estranged, her death in 1912 had a traumatic effect on him.

The only way to get rid of a temptation is to yield to it.

– Oscar Wilde (1854-1900). 'Chapter Two', from *The Picture of Dorian Gray* (1890) – Lord Henry speaking to the ever-youthful Dorian.

Then is Love blest, when from the cup of the body he drinks the wine of the soul.

– Richard Garnett (1835-1906), *De Flagello Myrtes: Thoughts and Fancies on Love* (1905).

FAMILIARITY BREEDS CONTEMPT — AND CHILDREN.

– Mark Twain (1835-1910), a jotting from *Mark Twain's Notebook.*

The tragedy of sexual intercourse is the perpetual virginity of the soul.

– William Butler Yeats (1865-1939), speaking after consummating his relationship with Maud Gonne, in Paris, in 1908. Yeats had previously been infatuated with Maud, seeing her as a confidant and muse – but the relationship faltered after that night.

Coitus is the punishment for the happiness of being together.

– Franz Kafka (1883-1924), *Kafka's Diary* – written shortly before a trip to Italy to see his fiancée Felice Bauer. Kafka had a very active sex life, and in fact was 'tortured' by sexual desire, noting in 1922 that 'sex keeps gnawing at me.' Although he never married, Kafka visited brothels for most of his adult life.

Now sex and beauty are one thing, like flame and fire. If you hate sex you hate beauty. If you love *living* beauty, you have a reverence for sex. Of course you can love old dead beauty and hate sex. But to love living beauty, you must have a reverence for sex.

Sex and beauty are inseparable, like life and consciousness. And the intelligence which goes with sex and beauty, and arises out of sex and beauty, is intuition.

– D.H. Lawrence (1885-1930), whose collected works, among other things, represent an extended reflection upon the dehumanising effects of modernity and industrialisation. In this essay, 'Sex Appeal, or Sex Locked Out' (1928), originally written for the *Sunday Dispatch,* a glimmer of hope is proffered.

There comes a moment in the day when you have written your pages in the morning, attended to your correspondence in the afternoon, and have nothing further to do. Then comes that hour when you are bored; that's the time for sex.

– H.G. Wells (1866-1946), the father of science fiction and author of *The War of the Worlds, The Invisible Man* and *The Island of Doctor Moreau.*

Poetry makes nothing happen.

– W.H. Auden

The Writers On… Series hopes to show that words, crafted well, with thought, precision and imagination, can have a lasting impact on the world around us.

A good quotation can illuminate meaning, provide evidence or inspiration, pay homage or merely make the user seem well-read.

But what is the importance of being 'well-read'? Literature, although pleasing and entertaining in itself, is so much more than that. Like all the creative arts, it preserves ideals, and is often the last thing left to speak across the ages. It makes the otherwise non-existent, un-envisaged, and un-spoken widely available. As W.H. Auden so aptly states, 'Poetry makes nothing happen.' And this nothingness is exactly the point. With the act of reading, good writing makes the previously un-imagined, *possible*. Through poetry and prose, nothing becomes something.

Dealing with any aspect of our daily lives, from serious topics such as love and the environment, to sensual pleasures such as food, drink or sex – it is good to bear in mind those words which have peaked our awareness. With this collection of some of the greatest, *Writers On...* the reader will hopefully never be short of possibilities.

Also in the *Writers On...* Series

WRITERS
ON ...
LOVE
AMELIA CARRUTHERS

WRITERS
ON ...
ATHEISM
AMELIA CARRUTHERS

WRITERS
ON ...
NATURE
AMELIA CARRUTHERS

WRITERS
ON ...
FOOD
AMELIA CARRUTHERS

Printed in Great Britain
by Amazon

20327202R00092